AMERICAN COMMUNITIES

We Live in a
CITY

Amy B. Rogers

PowerKiDS press™

New York

Published in 2016 by The Rosen Publishing Group, Inc.
29 East 21st Street, New York, NY 10010

First Edition

Editor: Katie Kawa
Book Design: Reann Nye

Photo Credits: Cover Kunal Mehta/Shutterstock.com; cover, pp. 3–24 (background texture) Evgeny Karandaev/Shutterstock.com; p. 5 © iStockphoto.com/ImageSource; p. 6 © iStockphoto.com/Kubrak78; pp. 9, 24 (skyscraper) Joseph Sohm/Shutterstock.com; p. 10 Beth Perkins/Taxi/Getty Images; pp. 13, 24 (apartment) Max Herman/Shutterstock.com; p. 14 Charles Cook/Lonely Planet Images/Getty Images; pp. 17, 24 (subway) © iStockphoto.com/Alex Potemkin; p. 18 Slava Lane Oatey/Blue Jean Images/Getty Images; p. 21 Bruce Leighty/Stockbyte/Getty Images; p. 22 Jaren Jai Wicklund/Shutterstock.com.

. Cataloging-in-Publication Data

Rogers, Amy B.
We live in a city / by Amy B. Rogers.
p. cm. — (American communities)
Includes index.
ISBN 978-1-5081-4189-1 (pbk.)
ISBN 978-1-5081-4190-7 (6-pack)
ISBN 978-1-5081-4191-4 (library binding)
1. Cities and towns — Juvenile literature. 2. Urban ecology (Sociology) — Juvenile literature. I. Rogers, Amy B. II. Title.
HT152.R58 2016
307.76—d23

Manufactured in the United States of America

CPSIA Compliance Information: Batch #BW16PK: For Further Information contact Rosen Publishing, New York, New York at 1-800-237-9932

Contents

We live in a city. A city is also known as an urban community.

Millions of people live in our city.

Our city has many tall buildings. The tallest buildings are called **skyscrapers**.

Many people in cities live in **apartment buildings**. An apartment is a group of rooms where people live.

One apartment building can hold many apartments.

14

Our city has many ways
to get from place to place.
Some people take the bus.

People can get around our city by using the **subway**. The subway is an underground train.

TRACK 2

2 Track

17

The buildings in our city are close together. We can walk to the store.

The leader of a city is called the mayor. Our mayor works at city hall.

21

A city is an exciting place to live!

Words to Know

apartment building

skyscrapers

subway

Index

Websites

Due to the changing nature of Internet links, PowerKids Press has developed an online list of websites related to the subject of this book. This site is updated regularly. Please use this link to access the list: www.powerkidslinks.com/acom/city